"You don't have whole staircase, just take the first step."

Martin Luther King

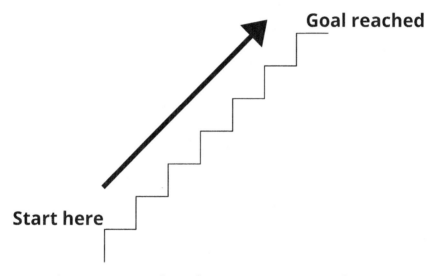

Goal reached

Start here

Simply move in the direction you wish to go...
one step at a time.

1. Be clear on what you want (**main goal**)
2. Take the **first step** toward your goal.
3. **Keep going**.
4. Reach your goal.

If you can **write down on paper** and **visualize** the steps you need to take, reaching your goal becomes easier. Do this, whether your goal is small or large, easy or hard.

Here's a simple example:

Let's say, it's your goal to get the laundry done today (**main goal**).

Required steps to reach main goal...

1. Gather up the dirty clothes.
2. Separate into appropriate color piles.
3. Choose one pile and put into washer.
4. Get the laundry detergent.
5. Pour the correct amount of laundry detergent into the washer dispenser.
6. Turn the washing machine on.
7. When cycle is finished, remove laundry to dryer.
8. Set dryer to appropriate drying time.
9. Remove dry laundry when cycle is finished and carry to flat surface for folding.
10. Fold laundry.
11. Put fresh, folded laundry away.

Keep Going.
Take Action
(most important)

Today's date--------------------

What is the one thing I want to accomplish today?

What is the first step I need to take?

If I can, I will take more steps (keep going)

1. --
2. --
3. --

Did I reach my original goal today?
- Yes
- Partly (keep going tomorrow)
- No (why?)

Don't
QUIT

-

Today's date-------------------

What is the one thing I want to accomplish today?

What is the first step I need to take?

If I can, I will take more steps (keep going)

1. --
2. --
3. --

Did I reach my original goal today?

- Yes
- Partly (keep going tomorrow)
- No (why?)

Don't
QUIT

-

Today's date-------------------

What is the one thing I want to accomplish today?

What is the first step I need to take?

If I can, I will take more steps (keep going)

1. --
2. --
3. --

Did I reach my original goal today?
- Yes
- Partly (keep going tomorrow)
- No (why?)

Don't
QUIT

-

Today's date-------------------

What is the one thing I want to accomplish today?

What is the first step I need to take?

If I can, I will take more steps (keep going)

1. ---
2. ---
3. ---

Did I reach my original goal today?
- Yes
- Partly (keep going tomorrow)
- No (why?)

Don't
QUIT

-

Today's date-------------------------

What is the one thing I want to accomplish today?

What is the first step I need to take?

If I can, I will take more steps (keep going)

1. ---
2. ---
3. ---

Did I reach my original goal today?
- Yes
- Partly (keep going tomorrow)
- No (why?)

Don't QUIT

-

Today's date--------------------

What is the one thing I want to accomplish today?

What is the first step I need to take?

If I can, I will take more steps (keep going)

1. --
2. --
3. --

Did I reach my original goal today?
- Yes
- Partly (keep going tomorrow)
- No (why?)

Don't
QUIT

-

Today's date--------------------

What is the one thing I want to accomplish today?

What is the first step I need to take?

If I can, I will take more steps (keep going)

1. --
2. --
3. --

Did I reach my original goal today?
- Yes
- Partly (keep going tomorrow)
- No (why?)

Don't
QUIT

-

Today's date------------------------

What is the one thing I want to accomplish today?

What is the first step I need to take?

If I can, I will take more steps (keep going)

1. --
2. --
3. --

Did I reach my original goal today?
- Yes
- Partly (keep going tomorrow)
- No (why?)

Don't
QUIT

-

Today's date-------------------

What is the one thing I want to accomplish today?

What is the first step I need to take?

If I can, I will take more steps (keep going)

1. ---
2. ---
3. ---

Did I reach my original goal today?
- Yes
- Partly (keep going tomorrow)
- No (why?)

Don't
QUIT

-

Today's date--------------------

What is the one thing I want to accomplish today?

What is the first step I need to take?

If I can, I will take more steps (keep going)

1. --
2. --
3. --

Did I reach my original goal today?
- Yes
- Partly (keep going tomorrow)
- No (why?)

Don't
QUIT

-

Today's date--------------------

What is the one thing I want to accomplish today?

What is the first step I need to take?

If I can, I will take more steps (keep going)

1. --
2. --
3. --

Did I reach my original goal today?
- Yes
- Partly (keep going tomorrow)
- No (why?)

Don't
QUIT

-

Today's date--------------------

What is the one thing I want to accomplish today?

What is the first step I need to take?

If I can, I will take more steps (keep going)

1. --
2. --
3. --

Did I reach my original goal today?
- Yes
- Partly (keep going tomorrow)
- No (why?)

Don't
QUIT

-

Today's date-------------------

What is the one thing I want to accomplish today?

What is the first step I need to take?

If I can, I will take more steps (keep going)

1. --
2. --
3. --

Did I reach my original goal today?
- Yes
- Partly (keep going tomorrow)
- No (why?)

Don't
QUIT

-

Today's date--------------------

What is the one thing I want to accomplish today?

What is the first step I need to take?

If I can, I will take more steps (keep going)

1. --
2. --
3. --

Did I reach my original goal today?
- Yes
- Partly (keep going tomorrow)
- No (why?)

Don't QUIT

-

Today's date--------------------

What is the one thing I want to accomplish today?

What is the first step I need to take?

If I can, I will take more steps (keep going)

1. --
2. --
3. --

Did I reach my original goal today?
- Yes
- Partly (keep going tomorrow)
- No (why?)

Don't
QUIT

-

Today's date-------------------------

What is the one thing I want to accomplish today?

What is the first step I need to take?

If I can, I will take more steps (keep going)

1. ---
2. ---
3. ---

Did I reach my original goal today?
- Yes
- Partly (keep going tomorrow)
- No (why?)

Don't
QUIT

-

Today's date--------------------------

What is the one thing I want to accomplish today?

What is the first step I need to take?

If I can, I will take more steps (keep going)

1. --
2. --
3. --

Did I reach my original goal today?
- Yes
- Partly (keep going tomorrow)
- No (why?)

Don't
QUIT

-

Today's date--------------------

What is the one thing I want to accomplish today?

What is the first step I need to take?

If I can, I will take more steps (keep going)

1. --
2. --
3. --

Did I reach my original goal today?
- Yes
- Partly (keep going tomorrow)
- No (why?)

Don't
QUIT

-

Today's date--------------------

What is the one thing I want to accomplish today?

What is the first step I need to take?

If I can, I will take more steps (keep going)

1. --
2. --
3. --

Did I reach my original goal today?
- Yes
- Partly (keep going tomorrow)
- No (why?)

Don't
QUIT

-

Today's date-------------------

What is the one thing I want to accomplish today?

What is the first step I need to take?

If I can, I will take more steps (keep going)

1. ---
2. ---
3. ---

Did I reach my original goal today?
- Yes
- Partly (keep going tomorrow)
- No (why?)

Don't
QUIT

-

Today's date-------------------

What is the one thing I want to accomplish today?

What is the first step I need to take?

If I can, I will take more steps (keep going)

1. --
2. --
3. --

Did I reach my original goal today?
- Yes
- Partly (keep going tomorrow)
- No (why?)

Don't
QUIT

-

Today's date--------------------

What is the one thing I want to accomplish today?

What is the first step I need to take?

If I can, I will take more steps (keep going)

1. --
2. --
3. --

Did I reach my original goal today?
- Yes
- Partly (keep going tomorrow)
- No (why?)

Don't
QUIT

-

Today's date-------------------

What is the one thing I want to accomplish today?

What is the first step I need to take?

If I can, I will take more steps (keep going)

1. --
2. --
3. --

Did I reach my original goal today?
- Yes
- Partly (keep going tomorrow)
- No (why?)

Don't
QUIT

-

Today's date--------------------

What is the one thing I want to accomplish today?

What is the first step I need to take?

If I can, I will take more steps (keep going)

1. ---
2. ---
3. ---

Did I reach my original goal today?
- Yes
- Partly (keep going tomorrow)
- No (why?)

Don't
QUIT

-

Today's date-------------------------

What is the one thing I want to accomplish today?

What is the first step I need to take?

If I can, I will take more steps (keep going)

1. ---
2. ---
3. ---

Did I reach my original goal today?
- Yes
- Partly (keep going tomorrow)
- No (why?)

Don't
QUIT

-

Today's date--------------------

What is the one thing I want to accomplish today?

What is the first step I need to take?

If I can, I will take more steps (keep going)

1. --
2. --
3. --

Did I reach my original goal today?
- Yes
- Partly (keep going tomorrow)
- No (why?)

Don't
QUIT

-

Today's date-------------------

What is the one thing I want to accomplish today?

What is the first step I need to take?

If I can, I will take more steps (keep going)

1. ---
2. ---
3. ---

Did I reach my original goal today?
- Yes
- Partly (keep going tomorrow)
- No (why?)

Don't
QUIT

-

Today's date-------------------

What is the one thing I want to accomplish today?

What is the first step I need to take?

If I can, I will take more steps (keep going)

1. ---
2. ---
3. ---

Did I reach my original goal today?
- Yes
- Partly (keep going tomorrow)
- No (why?)

Don't QUIT

-

Today's date-------------------

What is the one thing I want to accomplish today?

What is the first step I need to take?

If I can, I will take more steps (keep going)

1. --
2. --
3. --

Did I reach my original goal today?
- Yes
- Partly (keep going tomorrow)
- No (why?)

Don't
QUIT

-

Today's date--------------------

What is the one thing I want to accomplish today?

What is the first step I need to take?

If I can, I will take more steps (keep going)

1. --
2. --
3. --

Did I reach my original goal today?
- Yes
- Partly (keep going tomorrow)
- No (why?)

Don't
QUIT

-

Today's date------------------

What is the one thing I want to accomplish today?

What is the first step I need to take?

If I can, I will take more steps (keep going)

1. --
2. --
3. --

Did I reach my original goal today?
- Yes
- Partly (keep going tomorrow)
- No (why?)

Don't
QUIT

-

Today's date--------------------

What is the one thing I want to accomplish today?

What is the first step I need to take?

If I can, I will take more steps (keep going)

1. --
2. --
3. --

Did I reach my original goal today?
- Yes
- Partly (keep going tomorrow)
- No (why?)

Don't
QUIT

-

Today's date-------------------

What is the one thing I want to accomplish today?

What is the first step I need to take?

If I can, I will take more steps (keep going)

1. ---
2. ---
3. ---

Did I reach my original goal today?
- Yes
- Partly (keep going tomorrow)
- No (why?)

Don't
QUIT

-

Today's date--------------------

What is the one thing I want to accomplish today?

What is the first step I need to take?

If I can, I will take more steps (keep going)

1. --
2. --
3. --

Did I reach my original goal today?
- Yes
- Partly (keep going tomorrow)
- No (why?)

Don't
QUIT

-

Today's date--------------------

What is the one thing I want to accomplish today?

What is the first step I need to take?

If I can, I will take more steps (keep going)

1. --
2. --
3. --

Did I reach my original goal today?
- Yes
- Partly (keep going tomorrow)
- No (why?)

Don't *QUIT*

-

Today's date---------------------

What is the one thing I want to accomplish today?

What is the first step I need to take?

If I can, I will take more steps (keep going)

1. ---
2. ---
3. ---

Did I reach my original goal today?
- Yes
- Partly (keep going tomorrow)
- No (why?)

Don't
QUIT

-

Today's date----------------------

What is the one thing I want to accomplish today?

What is the first step I need to take?

If I can, I will take more steps (keep going)

1. ---
2. ---
3. ---

Did I reach my original goal today?
- Yes
- Partly (keep going tomorrow)
- No (why?)

Don't
QUIT

-

Today's date-------------------------

What is the one thing I want to accomplish today?

What is the first step I need to take?

If I can, I will take more steps (keep going)

1. ---
2. ---
3. ---

Did I reach my original goal today?
- Yes
- Partly (keep going tomorrow)
- No (why?)

Don't QUIT

-

Today's date--------------------

What is the one thing I want to accomplish today?

What is the first step I need to take?

If I can, I will take more steps (keep going)

1. --
2. --
3. --

Did I reach my original goal today?
- Yes
- Partly (keep going tomorrow)
- No (why?)

Don't
QUIT

-

Today's date-------------------

What is the one thing I want to accomplish today?

What is the first step I need to take?

If I can, I will take more steps (keep going)

1. --
2. --
3. --

Did I reach my original goal today?
- Yes
- Partly (keep going tomorrow)
- No (why?)

Don't
QUIT

-

Today's date--------------------

What is the one thing I want to accomplish today?

What is the first step I need to take?

If I can, I will take more steps (keep going)

1. --
2. --
3. --

Did I reach my original goal today?
- Yes
- Partly (keep going tomorrow)
- No (why?)

Don't
QUIT

-

Today's date-------------------

What is the one thing I want to accomplish today?

What is the first step I need to take?

If I can, I will take more steps (keep going)

1. --
2. --
3. --

Did I reach my original goal today?
- Yes
- Partly (keep going tomorrow)
- No (why?)

Don't
QUIT

-

Today's date-------------------

What is the one thing I want to accomplish today?

What is the first step I need to take?

If I can, I will take more steps (keep going)

1. ---
2. ---
3. ---

Did I reach my original goal today?

- Yes
- Partly (keep going tomorrow)
- No (why?)

Don't QUIT

-

Today's date--------------------

What is the one thing I want to accomplish today?

What is the first step I need to take?

If I can, I will take more steps (keep going)

1. ---
2. ---
3. ---

Did I reach my original goal today?
- Yes
- Partly (keep going tomorrow)
- No (why?)

Don't
QUIT

-

Today's date--------------------

What is the one thing I want to accomplish today?

What is the first step I need to take?

If I can, I will take more steps (keep going)

1. ---
2. ---
3. ---

Did I reach my original goal today?
- Yes
- Partly (keep going tomorrow)
- No (why?)

Don't
QUIT

-

Today's date-------------------

What is the one thing I want to accomplish today?

What is the first step I need to take?

If I can, I will take more steps (keep going)

1. ---
2. ---
3. ---

Did I reach my original goal today?
- Yes
- Partly (keep going tomorrow)
- No (why?)

Don't
QUIT

-

Today's date-------------------

What is the one thing I want to accomplish today?

What is the first step I need to take?

If I can, I will take more steps (keep going)

1. --
2. --
3. --

Did I reach my original goal today?

- Yes
- Partly (keep going tomorrow)
- No (why?)

Don't
QUIT

-

Today's date--------------------

What is the one thing I want to accomplish today?

What is the first step I need to take?

If I can, I will take more steps (keep going)

1. --
2. --
3. --

Did I reach my original goal today?
- Yes
- Partly (keep going tomorrow)
- No (why?)

Don't
QUIT

-

Today's date-------------------

What is the one thing I want to accomplish today?

What is the first step I need to take?

If I can, I will take more steps (keep going)

1. ---
2. ---
3. ---

Did I reach my original goal today?
- Yes
- Partly (keep going tomorrow)
- No (why?)

Don't
QUIT

-

Today's date-------------------

What is the one thing I want to accomplish today?

What is the first step I need to take?

If I can, I will take more steps (keep going)

1. --
2. --
3. --

Did I reach my original goal today?
- Yes
- Partly (keep going tomorrow)
- No (why?)

Don't
QUIT

-

Today's date-------------------

What is the one thing I want to accomplish today?

What is the first step I need to take?

If I can, I will take more steps (keep going)

1. --
2. --
3. --

Did I reach my original goal today?

- Yes
- Partly (keep going tomorrow)
- No (why?)

Don't
QUIT

-

Today's date--------------------

What is the one thing I want to accomplish today?

What is the first step I need to take?

If I can, I will take more steps (keep going)

1. --
2. --
3. --

Did I reach my original goal today?
- Yes
- Partly (keep going tomorrow)
- No (why?)

Don't
QUIT

-

Today's date-------------------

What is the one thing I want to accomplish today?

What is the first step I need to take?

If I can, I will take more steps (keep going)

1. --
2. --
3. --

Did I reach my original goal today?
- Yes
- Partly (keep going tomorrow)
- No (why?)

Don't
QUIT

-

Today's date-------------------

What is the one thing I want to accomplish today?

What is the first step I need to take?

If I can, I will take more steps (keep going)

1. --
2. --
3. --

Did I reach my original goal today?
- Yes
- Partly (keep going tomorrow)
- No (why?)

Don't
QUIT

-

Today's date--------------------

What is the one thing I want to accomplish today?

What is the first step I need to take?

If I can, I will take more steps (keep going)

1. ---
2. ---
3. ---

Did I reach my original goal today?
- Yes
- Partly (keep going tomorrow)
- No (why?)

Don't
QUIT

-

Today's date-------------------

What is the one thing I want to accomplish today?

What is the first step I need to take?

If I can, I will take more steps (keep going)

1. ---
2. ---
3. ---

Did I reach my original goal today?
- Yes
- Partly (keep going tomorrow)
- No (why?)

Don't
QUIT

-

Today's date--------------------------

What is the one thing I want to accomplish today?

What is the first step I need to take?

If I can, I will take more steps (keep going)

1. --
2. --
3. --

Did I reach my original goal today?
- Yes
- Partly (keep going tomorrow)
- No (why?)

Don't QUIT

-

Today's date-------------------

What is the one thing I want to accomplish today?

What is the first step I need to take?

If I can, I will take more steps (keep going)

1. --
2. --
3. --

Did I reach my original goal today?
- Yes
- Partly (keep going tomorrow)
- No (why?)

Don't
QUIT

-

Today's date-------------------

What is the one thing I want to accomplish today?

What is the first step I need to take?

If I can, I will take more steps (keep going)

1. --
2. --
3. --

Did I reach my original goal today?
- Yes
- Partly (keep going tomorrow)
- No (why?)

Don't
QUIT

-

Today's date-------------------

What is the one thing I want to accomplish today?

What is the first step I need to take?

If I can, I will take more steps (keep going)

1. --
2. --
3. --

Did I reach my original goal today?
- Yes
- Partly (keep going tomorrow)
- No (why?)

Don't
QUIT

-

Today's date--------------------

What is the one thing I want to accomplish today?

What is the first step I need to take?

If I can, I will take more steps (keep going)

1. --
2. --
3. --

Did I reach my original goal today?
- Yes
- Partly (keep going tomorrow)
- No (why?)

Don't
QUIT

-

Today's date--------------------

What is the one thing I want to accomplish today?

What is the first step I need to take?

If I can, I will take more steps (keep going)

1. ---
2. ---
3. ---

Did I reach my original goal today?
- Yes
- Partly (keep going tomorrow)
- No (why?)

Don't
QUIT

-

Today's date-------------------

What is the one thing I want to accomplish today?

What is the first step I need to take?

If I can, I will take more steps (keep going)

1. ---
2. ---
3. ---

Did I reach my original goal today?
- Yes
- Partly (keep going tomorrow)
- No (why?)

Don't
QUIT

-

Today's date--------------------

What is the one thing I want to accomplish today?

What is the first step I need to take?

If I can, I will take more steps (keep going)

1. --
2. --
3. --

Did I reach my original goal today?
- Yes
- Partly (keep going tomorrow)
- No (why?)

Don't
QUIT

-

Today's date-------------------

What is the one thing I want to accomplish today?

What is the first step I need to take?

If I can, I will take more steps (keep going)

1. --
2. --
3. --

Did I reach my original goal today?

- Yes
- Partly (keep going tomorrow)
- No (why?)

Don't
QUIT

-

Today's date--------------------

What is the one thing I want to accomplish today?

What is the first step I need to take?

If I can, I will take more steps (keep going)

1. --
2. --
3. --

Did I reach my original goal today?
- Yes
- Partly (keep going tomorrow)
- No (why?)

Don't
QUIT

-

Today's date-------------------

What is the one thing I want to accomplish today?

What is the first step I need to take?

If I can, I will take more steps (keep going)

1. ---
2. ---
3. ---

Did I reach my original goal today?
- Yes
- Partly (keep going tomorrow)
- No (why?)

Don't QUIT

-

Today's date--------------------

What is the one thing I want to accomplish today?

What is the first step I need to take?

If I can, I will take more steps (keep going)

1. --
2. --
3. --

Did I reach my original goal today?
- Yes
- Partly (keep going tomorrow)
- No (why?)

Don't
QUIT

-

Today's date-------------------

What is the one thing I want to accomplish today?

What is the first step I need to take?

If I can, I will take more steps (keep going)

1. --
2. --
3. --

Did I reach my original goal today?
- Yes
- Partly (keep going tomorrow)
- No (why?)

Don't
QUIT

-

Today's date--------------------

What is the one thing I want to accomplish today?

What is the first step I need to take?

If I can, I will take more steps (keep going)

1. ---
2. ---
3. ---

Did I reach my original goal today?
- Yes
- Partly (keep going tomorrow)
- No (why?)

Don't
QUIT

-

Today's date--------------------

What is the one thing I want to accomplish today?

What is the first step I need to take?

If I can, I will take more steps (keep going)

1. --
2. --
3. --

Did I reach my original goal today?
- Yes
- Partly (keep going tomorrow)
- No (why?)

Don't
QUIT

-

Today's date-------------------

What is the one thing I want to accomplish today?

What is the first step I need to take?

If I can, I will take more steps (keep going)

1. --
2. --
3. --

Did I reach my original goal today?
- Yes
- Partly (keep going tomorrow)
- No (why?)

Don't
QUIT

-

Today's date--------------------

What is the one thing I want to accomplish today?

What is the first step I need to take?

If I can, I will take more steps (keep going)

1. --
2. --
3. --

Did I reach my original goal today?
- Yes
- Partly (keep going tomorrow)
- No (why?)

Don't
QUIT

-

Today's date--------------------

What is the one thing I want to accomplish today?

What is the first step I need to take?

If I can, I will take more steps (keep going)

1. --
2. --
3. --

Did I reach my original goal today?

- Yes
- Partly (keep going tomorrow)
- No (why?)

Don't
QUIT

-

Today's date-------------------------

What is the one thing I want to accomplish today?

What is the first step I need to take?

If I can, I will take more steps (keep going)

1. ---
2. ---
3. ---

Did I reach my original goal today?
- Yes
- Partly (keep going tomorrow)
- No (why?)

Don't
QUIT

-

Today's date-------------------

What is the one thing I want to accomplish today?

What is the first step I need to take?

If I can, I will take more steps (keep going)

1. --
2. --
3. --

Did I reach my original goal today?
- Yes
- Partly (keep going tomorrow)
- No (why?)

Don't
QUIT

-

Today's date-------------------

What is the one thing I want to accomplish today?

What is the first step I need to take?

If I can, I will take more steps (keep going)

1. ---
2. ---
3. ---

Did I reach my original goal today?
- Yes
- Partly (keep going tomorrow)
- No (why?)

Don't
QUIT

-

Today's date-------------------------

What is the one thing I want to accomplish today?

What is the first step I need to take?

If I can, I will take more steps (keep going)

1. ---
2. ---
3. ---

Did I reach my original goal today?
- Yes
- Partly (keep going tomorrow)
- No (why?)

Don't
QUIT

-

Today's date------------------

What is the one thing I want to accomplish today?

What is the first step I need to take?

If I can, I will take more steps (keep going)

1. ---
2. ---
3. ---

Did I reach my original goal today?
- Yes
- Partly (keep going tomorrow)
- No (why?)

Don't
QUIT

-

Today's date--------------------

What is the one thing I want to accomplish today?

What is the first step I need to take?

If I can, I will take more steps (keep going)

1. ---
2. ---
3. ---

Did I reach my original goal today?

- Yes
- Partly (keep going tomorrow)
- No (why?)

Don't
QUIT

-

Today's date--------------------

What is the one thing I want to accomplish today?

What is the first step I need to take?

If I can, I will take more steps (keep going)

1. ---
2. ---
3. ---

Did I reach my original goal today?
- Yes
- Partly (keep going tomorrow)
- No (why?)

Don't
QUIT

-

Today's date-------------------------

What is the one thing I want to accomplish today?

What is the first step I need to take?

If I can, I will take more steps (keep going)

1. --
2. --
3. --

Did I reach my original goal today?
- Yes
- Partly (keep going tomorrow)
- No (why?)

Don't QUIT

-

Today's date--------------------

What is the one thing I want to accomplish today?

What is the first step I need to take?

If I can, I will take more steps (keep going)

1. --
2. --
3. --

Did I reach my original goal today?
- Yes
- Partly (keep going tomorrow)
- No (why?)

Don't QUIT

-

Today's date--------------------

What is the one thing I want to accomplish today?

What is the first step I need to take?

If I can, I will take more steps (keep going)

1. ---
2. ---
3. ---

Did I reach my original goal today?

- Yes
- Partly (keep going tomorrow)
- No (why?)

Don't
QUIT

-

Today's date------------------------

What is the one thing I want to accomplish today?

What is the first step I need to take?

If I can, I will take more steps (keep going)

1. --
2. --
3. --

Did I reach my original goal today?
- Yes
- Partly (keep going tomorrow)
- No (why?)

Don't QUIT

-

Today's date-------------------

What is the one thing I want to accomplish today?

What is the first step I need to take?

If I can, I will take more steps (keep going)

1. ---
2. ---
3. ---

Did I reach my original goal today?
- Yes
- Partly (keep going tomorrow)
- No (why?)

Don't
QUIT

-

Today's date-------------------

What is the one thing I want to accomplish today?

What is the first step I need to take?

If I can, I will take more steps (keep going)

1. ---
2. ---
3. ---

Did I reach my original goal today?
- Yes
- Partly (keep going tomorrow)
- No (why?)

Don't QUIT

-

Today's date-------------------

What is the one thing I want to accomplish today?

What is the first step I need to take?

If I can, I will take more steps (keep going)

1. ---
2. ---
3. ---

Did I reach my original goal today?
- Yes
- Partly (keep going tomorrow)
- No (why?)

Don't QUIT

-

Today's date-------------------

What is the one thing I want to accomplish today?

What is the first step I need to take?

If I can, I will take more steps (keep going)

1. --
2. --
3. --

Did I reach my original goal today?
- Yes
- Partly (keep going tomorrow)
- No (why?)

Don't
QUIT

-

Today's date-------------------

What is the one thing I want to accomplish today?

What is the first step I need to take?

If I can, I will take more steps (keep going)

1. ---
2. ---
3. ---

Did I reach my original goal today?
- Yes
- Partly (keep going tomorrow)
- No (why?)

Don't
QUIT

-

Today's date-------------------

What is the one thing I want to accomplish today?

What is the first step I need to take?

If I can, I will take more steps (keep going)

1. --
2. --
3. --

Did I reach my original goal today?
- Yes
- Partly (keep going tomorrow)
- No (why?)

Don't
QUIT

-

Today's date--------------------

What is the one thing I want to accomplish today?

What is the first step I need to take?

If I can, I will take more steps (keep going)

1. ---
2. ---
3. ---

Did I reach my original goal today?
- Yes
- Partly (keep going tomorrow)
- No (why?)

Don't
QUIT

-

Today's date---------------------

What is the one thing I want to accomplish today?

What is the first step I need to take?

If I can, I will take more steps (keep going)

1. --
2. --
3. --

Did I reach my original goal today?
- Yes
- Partly (keep going tomorrow)
- No (why?)

Don't
QUIT

-

Today's date------------------

What is the one thing I want to accomplish today?

What is the first step I need to take?

If I can, I will take more steps (keep going)

1. --
2. --
3. --

Did I reach my original goal today?
- Yes
- Partly (keep going tomorrow)
- No (why?)

Don't QUIT

-

Today's date-------------------

What is the one thing I want to accomplish today?

What is the first step I need to take?

If I can, I will take more steps (keep going)

1. ---
2. ---
3. ---

Did I reach my original goal today?
- Yes
- Partly (keep going tomorrow)
- No (why?)

Don't
QUIT

-

Today's date-------------------

What is the one thing I want to accomplish today?

What is the first step I need to take?

If I can, I will take more steps (keep going)

1. --
2. --
3. --

Did I reach my original goal today?
- Yes
- Partly (keep going tomorrow) Don't
- No (why?) QUIT

-

The End

...but not really.
Keep going.

I hope you enjoyed your
Motivate Me
Notebook/Journaling
experience.
I hope it helped you to clarify
your wants, whys and how tos.

Here's to you!

Printed in Great Britain
by Amazon